Victorian and Edwardian EDINBURGH

from old photographs

D0186238

1 *The Heart of the Royal Mile, c.* 1890. The view takes in the meeting point of Edinburgh and the Canongate – created a burgh of regality in favour of the Augustine canons of Holyrood by King David I in 1128. The name derives from the old Saxon word *gaet* or way of the canons and the burgh retained its separate existence and administration for over 700 years until 1856. The streets which cross at the Netherbow Port referred to at No. 19, formerly St Mary's Wynd and Leith Wynd, follow the line of an ancient Roman thoroughfare

Victorian and Edwardian
EDINBURGH
from old photographs

Introduction and commentaries by
C. S. MINTO

B. T. BATSFORD LTD
LONDON

First published 1973
First paperback edition 1976
Text © C. S. Minto 1973

Printed in Great Britain by litho by
The Anchor Press Ltd and bound by
Wm Brendon & Son Ltd, both of Tiptree, Essex
for the publishers
B. T. Batsford Ltd,
4 Fitzhardinge Street,
London W1H 0AH

ISBN 0 7134 0333 0

CONTENTS

ACKNOWLEDGMENTS

This selection of photographs could not have been made without the active help and co-operation of my successor in office as City Librarian and Curator of Edinburgh and it is to him and to his staff in the local history departments of the Libraries and Museums service that first acknowledgments are due. Most of the photographs, over 80 per cent of the whole, were found in the Edinburgh Room and Huntly House Museum collections, but private sources have also been of inestimable value in providing variety and extending coverage with previously unpublished examples. Miss M. Rhodes, Miss M. Ritchie, Mrs A. Ross, Messrs H. Annan, W. G. Lush, J. C. Miller and R. G. Smith and a lady who prefers to remain anonymous have all offered unfettered use of family albums or other collections. In the selection process it has unfortunately not been found possible to use some of the material so generously offered, but we are none the less grateful on that account particularly as, on the principle that 'it's nae loss what a freen gets' all of these lenders willingly gave permission for the local history departments above mentioned to receive copies of any photographs that would fill gaps in their collections.

Specimens from Miss Rhodes' album can be seen at Nos. 8, 9, 17, 21, 23, 54, 66 and 68; from Mr Miller's at Nos. 26, 27, 69, 87, 91, 152, 153 and 154; and from 'anon' at Nos. 106, 119, 121 and 124. Single items have come from Mr Lush, No. 127, and Mr Smith, No. 104. To all these sources of new and, for the most part, unusual material the author of the commentaries, whose job it was to supply the photographs, and the publishers feel themselves very much indebted and take pleasure in recording their thanks. They are grateful, too, to the publishers of a number of recent books for permission to include portraits in the 'Famous Sons' section of the present volume – to Messrs Hart-Davis and Eric Quayle, Esq. for No. 76; American Telephone and Telegraph Company for No. 77; John Murray (Publishers) Ltd for No. 79; *Collier's Encyclopaedia,* World Publishing, 1967 edition for No. 80; *The Scotsman* and Leslie Frewin for No. 82; David Winter & Son Limited for No. 83. The Heart of Midlothian Football Club has also given permission for the reproduction of No. 128 from their book *The Story of the Hearts.*

INTRODUCTION

'There is no Edinburgh emigrant, far or near, from China to Peru, but he or she carries some lively pictures of the mind, some sunset behind the Castle cliffs, some snow scene, some maze of city lamps, indelible in the memory and delightful to study in the intervals of toil. For any such, if this book fall in their way, here are a few more home pictures. It would be pleasant if they should recognise a house where they had dwelt or a walk that they had taken.'

R. L. Stevenson: 'Edinburgh'.

Shortly after 1840 there came into existence one of the earliest of all photographic societies – the Edinburgh Calotype Club. The membership was drawn largely from the legal and medical professions and one of the Club's albums survives. Unfortunately the chemistry of the photographic processes was not sufficiently established in those early days for any of the prints to be suitable for the present volume, but the Club did lay the foundation of a tradition of photographic societies in the town that has contributed much to the pictorial record of the city. Calotype exposures were long – roughly four minutes or even more in bright sunshine – and figures were normally lacking in the prints produced. Indeed, it was not until the introduction of the 'wet-collodion' process by Scott Archer in 1851 that exposures became short enough to record even moderate movement with adequate sharpness. No. 41, one of the earliest photographs in the book, shows the difficulty that vehicles and pedestrians in motion presented to the photographer even after 1851.

The principles of photography – literally, drawing with light – were, of course, well known some centuries before J. L. M. Daguerre and W. H. Fox Talbot almost simultaneously published details of their respective processes in 1839. Daguerre used a metal plate coated with silver iodide to produce a single picture of excellent clarity and permanence, but the method was applied principally, though not exclusively, in the production of portraits. By contrast Fox Talbot's 'photogenic drawing' technique produced a negative on paper sensitised with chloride of silver from which as many positive prints as were required could be made. The results were known as 'calotypes' from the Greek word for beauty and it is this process that is the basis of almost all Victorian and Edwardian photography though glass and, later, celluloid film were not long in ousting paper as negative base material for general purposes. The early calotypes, however, had a beauty of image all their own that, in spite of the length of the exposures involved, so endeared it to many workers as to ensure the continued use of the process even after the invention of the dry plate in 1871 did away with the need to prepare the negative as shortly as possible before exposure in the camera. Even as late as 1910 there were three long-established professional photographers in Edinburgh advertising themselves as 'also calotypist', but few amateurs had not by then been won over by the convenience of plates and films. Calotype photographs can be seen at Nos. 55, 84, 110 and 115. These, and hundreds of others, owe their existence to the fortuitous forming of the most famous technician/artist collaboration in photographic history between Robert Adamson and David Octavius Hill. Adamson, already expert in the new art along with his elder brother Dr John Adamson through association with Professor Brewster at St Andrews, came to Edinburgh in 1843 to establish a photographic studio. He found premises on the southern slopes of the Calton Hill and was joined there in 1844 by Hill after the artist had interested a number of well known citizens and churchmen in a project dear to his heart. This project was for a painting of the signing of the 'Deed of Demission' which followed the 'Disruption' of the Church of Scotland in 1843 when over 450 members of the General Assembly of the Church broke away to form the Free Church of Scotland. A stand was taken on the principle of non-interference by the state in church government and great courage was shown by the ministers concerned in sacrificing their livings and their stipends. What concerns us, however, in the present connection is that Hill, in order to obtain likenesses for his painting, embarked on the photographic activity that has brought him lasting fame.

The studio on the Calton Hill was occupied as a residence by Hill after his partner's untimely death in 1848 until his own death in 1869. It then passed into the hands of Archibald Burns who had published in the previous year *Picturesque Bits from Old Edinburgh,* a small volume of photographs with a text by Thomas Henderson. Alex. A. Inglis bought the business in 1876 and took over 'Rock House', as the studio was by then known about 1880. It remained with the Inglis family, father, son and grandson until 1945, when the property was sold, so bringing to an end an existence of over a century as a photographic studio. During the Burns and A. A. Inglis periods of occupancy a now indeterminable number of photographs of the city were taken, but some measure of the extent of the studio's activity may be gauged from over 600 of the original glass plates now preserved, by courtesy of a later head of the firm, in the Central Public Library. Identifiable Inglis photographs are included at Nos. 3, 5, 16, 53, 126, 136 and 145, but it is suspected that a number of others, particularly some copied from old lantern slides of the period, are also of Inglis origin.

The Calton Hill studio was far from being alone in recording how Edinburgh looked between about 1870 and 1910 as the two big national firms, G. W. Wilson of Aberdeen and Valentine's of Dundee were also active in the capital during this period, as were several other local photographers. Notable among these were J. G. Tunny (Nos. 41 and 148); J. McKean (No. 63); John Patrick (Nos. 116 and 147); and James Patrick, 45 of whose photographs were used to illustrate the 1900 edition of John Geddie's *Romantic Edinburgh* (Nos. 12, 20 and 47). A number of the primarily portrait studios, of which there were from 30 to 50 or more at various times during the period with which we are concerned, also made occasional excursions outdoors so that there was no lack of professional activity. Among local firms making and marketing lantern slides were A. H. Baird, James Buncle, J. Lizars and T. J. Walls. Each had a considerable and fluctuating list of subjects. Such slides have been a fruitful, if difficult to reproduce, source of photographs as quite a number have been found without corresponding prints being traceable. Behind all this professionalism there ranged uncountable amateurs acting either individually or in groups, through camera clubs such as the Edinburgh Photographic Society which had a very active survey section for many years around the turn of the century. Some of the results of amateur enthusiasm have been referred to in the 'Acknowledgments' and photographs from a few known amateur sources are there noted. Here, however, mention should be made of one amateur whose considerable output is embodied in small part in a volume of prints in the Edinburgh Room and in much larger part in an extensive collection of his negatives also preserved there. He was Dr F. M. Chrystal, son of the Professor George Chrystal referred to in the caption of No. 132 and his services were much in demand by local historians. Some examples of his photographs can be seen at Nos. 7, 24, 29, 31, 33, 40, 71–75, 92, 108, 125, 131 and 138.

Throughout the gathering of material for *Victorian and Edwardian Edinburgh* a conscious effort has been made to present a fresh collection, the aim (happily achieved) being to offer twice as many prints as were required in order to create a reasonable basis for choice. Thus, none of the photographs used for the Edinburgh section of *Victorian and Edwardian Scotland* has been repeated and for similar reasons permission has not been sought to reproduce any of the items contributed since the publication of the earlier volume to the *Edinburgh Evening News* feature 'The Old Days'. Many interesting photographs taken in and around Edinburgh in Victorian and Edwardian times were brought to light in this feature but there seemed little justification for repeated publication so soon after their being before the public. It is thought, however, that readers of this book unfamiliar with the newspaper series might wish to know of it.

The sources of the photographs have varied from the obvious – published collections of views – to reports of local authority departments, specialist publications of one kind or another and privately owned collections, to the city's own extensive collection of over 90,000 pictorial items, comprising prints, photographs, lantern slides and photographic negatives. The culling through of this intimidating mass of material in the Central Public Library's Edinburgh Room has been an exhausting but always pleasureable task made at all times easier by preterhumanly helpful assistants and it is hoped that the end result will, in its turn, give pleasure to its readers. There are gaps that it would have been pleasant to fill, industrial scenes showing men and women at work being difficult to come by, but it is felt that the selection of photographs offered is reasonably representative of city (and country) life. This introduction begins with a quotation from R. L. Stevenson's 'Edinburgh' and it has been found remarkable how the truth of the same author's description of his native place as 'not so much a small city as the largest of small towns' has come ever more vividly alive during the course of the work. Where but in a small town would one expect, or hope, to be so intimately in contact with the countryside, to have countryside activities, scents and smells so constantly in the background of consciousness? Twentieth-century Edinburgh has crept steadily nearer to the foothills of the breezy Pentlands that Stevenson knew and loved so well; wide areas that were open land in his day have disappeared under houses, factories and roads, but nothing can rob the capital city of Holyrood Park – an enclosed expanse of mountain and loch since it was first fenced in 1544 – or of the hill and seaside areas within its boundaries. Such scenes as those depicted in photographs 116, 119–121, 124, 144 and 147 would not seem too unreal even today. An air of *rus in urbe* is yet present in our still fortunate town. Perhaps this growing series of books 'from old photographs' will help the realisation that much of what has disappeared was worth preserving and that the diminishing countryside near our cities is in ever more urgent need of protection.

In ending on a practical and personal note I would like to try to add something to the appreciation of the photographs in this book and of the difficulties under which many of them must have been obtained. It has been my fortunate lot since retirement to be engaged on the compilation of this book of pictures of what has been my home city for all but six months of my infant existence and I attribute my lifelong interest in the period of photography covered by it to the fact that, but for a year or two's delay in production I might myself have been in a position to contribute to it. Alas, at the end of King Edward's reign I was only beginning to importune long-suffering parents, relatives and family friends to be allowed to take their photographs and to roam around 'snapping', though that is hardly the operative word, my immediate surroundings which were on what was then the southern-most limits of the city. An early 'success' was to picture a German Zeppelin over the houses facing us in 1916.

I clearly remember the primitive but quite effective and well-loved piece of apparatus which was used on that occasion. I had had it for some five years though its date of birth was around the turn of the century and I had been given it for my tenth birthday. It took the form of a rectangular box some $10 \times 8 \times 4\frac{1}{2}$ inches in which was contained up to 24 glass plates in metal sheaths which were allowed to fall forward after – or occasionally *before* – exposure by the operation of a lever which also counted the number of exposures made. Its weight was considerable and seemed to grow disproportionately as the day wore on but it was as nothing when compared with the loads carried 50 or 60 years earlier by the photographers, professional and amateur, who left behind them many of the illustrations in this volume. In the 'wet collodion' period briefly mentioned earlier in particular not only had the cameras and plates themselves to be carried but also the means for coating and developing the latter. Special mobile darkrooms on wheels were commonly resorted to and minimum ancillary equipment was a voluminous light-proof changing bag. The plates had to be made sensitive to light as short a time as possible before exposure and developed as soon as possible thereafter. A supply of chemicals and fresh water was the order of the day. This was before enlargement from small negatives became the rule and 'Landscape' prints varied from half-plate ($6\frac{1}{2} \times 4\frac{3}{4}$ inches) up through whole-plate ($8\frac{1}{2} \times 6\frac{1}{2}$ inches) and even larger. Frequently several or all of these sizes could be produced in the same camera by the use of the appropriate plate holders and an average sort of size for a bellows camera ready for use would be 15×12 inches or considerably more with the bellows fully extended. The size of the negative on which I cut my photographic teeth was quarter-plate ($4\frac{1}{4} \times 3\frac{1}{4}$ inches). The camera could hardly have been called precision-built, but with all its apparent disadvantages by modern standards it worked well most of the time and would no doubt still be serviceable had I not dismembered it to use the parts to make an enlarger which in the end failed miserably to fit into the cupboard under the stair which was my improvised dark room. However, I could use it after dark on short winter days, to the detriment or, more frequently, elimination of the night's home work. D. and P. services were available even then of course but impecunious amateurs did their own and at least this one liked it.

THE ROYAL MILE

2 *View from the Castle* showing the eastern half of Princes Street, the National Gallery, the Royal Scottish Academy, the Scott Monument, the Calton Hill, the North Bridge and the Bank of Scotland on the Mound as they appeared in the mid-1860s

From its highest point on the Castle Rock the Royal Mile descends the ridge of the 'Old Town' of Edinburgh to Holyrood House, the Palace built in the early years of the sixteenth century alongside the ancient and now ruinous Abbey for King James the Fourth. The name is appropriate for, although it is now some 370 years since James the Sixth of Scotland and First of England last journeyed there, the street has witnessed many royal progresses since the two kingdoms were united. Therefore, even if by the period covered in this book Princes Street had stolen some of the ancient thoroughfare's processional thunder, 'The Mile' is the natural street in which to begin any view of the city. Here is the Edinburgh that would have been most familiar to visitor and citizen alike in Victorian and Edwardian times.

Though many of the old lands and houses had disappeared before Victoria ascended the throne and more were to vanish during her, and her son's, reigns, fortunately enough was then and has since been done by way of preservation and restoration to ensure that the character of the street can be visualised by a no more than moderate exercise of the imagination.

In general the sequence of the photographs is from the Castle downwards to Holyrood in sections roughly embraced by the Castlehill and the Lawnmarket, the High Street, and the Canongate.

3 *The Castle Esplanade* with a military parade in progress, *c.* 1895

4 *'Cannonball House'* at the head of the Castlehill built about 1630 and so named after a ball fired from the Half-Moon Battery of the Castle had lodged in its gable during the garrison's efforts to relieve the blockade set up by the forces of Prince Charles Edward Stuart, 'Bonnie Prince Charlie', in 1745. Photograph *c.* 1900

6 *Riddle's Close,* one of many on the south side of the Lawnmarket. The gateway on the right leads through to Riddle's Court and the house of Bailie Macmorran, a wealthy city merchant, who was shot and met his death in 1595 while exercising his duty as a magistrate in trying to secure the surrender of a recalcitrant band of High School pupils who had barricaded themselves into the school in pursuit of their demands for a holiday which they thought was their due. Student protest carried to extremes would seem to be nothing new! Photograph *c.* 1905

7 *The South side of the Lawnmarket, c.* 1911. Typical tenements with the clothes drying poles projecting into the street from many of the windows and the coal seller going about his unenviable job of delivery up steep and narrow stairs

8 *(opposite)* *The Royal Mile from the Outlook Tower, c.* 1905, showing the Lawnmarket, the George IV Bridge crossing, and the High Street with St Giles' Cathedral and the Tron Church prominent on the right

5 *(previous page)* *A typical seventeenth-century building, the Duke of Gordon's house* on the Castlehill, seen, about 1890, from Johnston Terrace, a nineteenth-century roadway which cut across the gardens of the Castlehill properties

9 *Milne's or Mylne's Court* built about 1690 by Robert Mylne, seventh in line of a famous family of royal master-masons. Photograph *c.* 1906

10 *The North side of the Lawnmarket, c.* 1875. The double-pedimented building in the centre, built about 1630, is Gladstone's Land, now restored and occupied by the Saltire Society, an organisation concerned with the promotion of the arts in Scotland. To the left are the entrances to Lady Stair's and Milne's Closes, the former housing a museum devoted to Burns, Scott and Stevenson. The museum building (Lady Stair's House) is of similar date to Gladstone's Land

11 *All Hallows' Horse Fair in the Grassmarket,* about 1890. This annual event had a long history, some early maps naming the Grassmarket as Horse Market Street

12 *The High Street and Lawnmarket* from St Giles' looking towards the Castle. The boy in the foreground is contemplating 'the Heart of Midlothian' set in stones in the pavement to mark the site of the Old Tolbooth or Jail demolished in 1817

13 *The Castle from the Grassmarket* in 1880. The Grassmarket, a recognised market since 1477, is still to some extent the carriers' quarter of the Old Town. At its eastern end was the old Corn Market and also the principal place of public execution, · the last execution taking place in 1784

14 *The cliff-like nature of the Old Town buildings,* determined by the steepness of the sides of the ridge of the Royal Mile is very evident in this photograph from Princes Street Gardens about 1860. Prominent on the left is the north face of the Royal Exchange, completed in 1761 and used as the City Chambers since 1811. Below the crown of St Giles' Cathedral the narrowness and depth of the old 'closes' is clearly seen

15 *The Sales.* A store at the corner of High Street and North Bridge holds its ever popular summer sale. Though this photograph is a little later than 1911 this particular sale was firmly established some years before and the queues are typical

16 *The City Chambers* became, as noted in the caption to No. 14, the seat of city government in 1811. The shops in the arches and within the quadrangle were swept away shortly after this photograph was taken. Photograph *c.* 1900

18 *A 'Child Garden' in Chessel's Court* in the Canongate about 1905, one of several charitable efforts to mitigate the discomforts of life in an overcrowded community. Chessel's Court has been restored by the Corporation in recent years

17 *(opposite)* *Looking up the High Street* in the opposite direction to No. 8 and taken at the same time. The distant spire is of the Tolbooth St John's Church where the General Assembly of the Church of Scotland met before the Assembly's hall on the Mound was built

19 *John Knox's House* in 1880. Not far beyond this house in which, by tradition, the great reformer lived for some time in the 1560s lies the end of the High Street. The site of the Netherbow Port, the gateway between the Royal Burgh of Edinburgh and the Burgh of Canongate, can be seen outlined in the surface of the street

20 *Moray House and the Canongate, c.* 1900. Built in the first quarter of the seventeenth century Moray House is more palatial in style than other contemporary Canongate buildings and is now incorporated in a teachers' training college. It was in 1650 that the Duke of Argyll witnessed from the prominent balcony the discomfiture of his arch-enemy Montrose on his way to execution at Edinburgh Cross. Cromwell lodged here in 1648

21 *Huntly House, c.* 1907. Now perhaps the most satisfactory of the restorations of noblemen's houses in the Royal Mile, the photograph shows 'the speaking house', so called from the motto tablets set into the walls, at a time when it was occupied by many families. The 'Song and Ballad Shop' popularly known as the Poet's Box sold broadsheets and the last of the Scottish chapbooks

22 *(opposite)* *The White Horse Close, c.* 1900. Dating from 1623 the White Horse Inn was for long the departure point of the London stage coach. The building and courtyard have recently been restored

23 *(opposite)* *The Canongate Church and the Burgh Cross,* c. 1906. The gable is surmounted by the burgh's crest, a stag's head and cross, commemorating the legendary delivery of King David the First from the attack of an enraged stag by the appearance in his hand of a miraculous cross. The cross was preserved in Holyrood Abbey until taken to Durham in 1346

24 *The Abbey Strand, Holyrood,* in 1903. The line-up of children marks the boundary of the Canongate and of the Sanctuary of the Abbey. Beyond this line debtors were assured of freedom from prosecution for 24 hours–48 hours if sanctuary was sought on a Saturday

25 *The Canongate Tolbooth or Burgh Court House and Jail, c.* 1907. Built at the end of the sixteenth century the Tolbooth is now restored as one of the City Museums and contains an important collection of Highland Dress and the Tartan in addition to local relics. As the Canongate Institute, the building played an important part in Canongate social life in Edwardian times

26 *Holyrood Palace forecourt, c.* 1907. The Royal Park, which includes the city's highest hill, lies beyond. This hill is known as Arthur's Seat (813 feet) but the derivation of the name is obscure, any connection with the legendary King Arthur being now generally discounted

27 *Members of the Royal Company of Archers* lined up on the wall of Holyrood Palace Garden, *c.* 1905. Chartered as a Royal Company by Queen Anne in 1704 the Archers have since been known as the King's (or Queen's) Bodyguard for Scotland and take precedence over all royal guards and troops of the line. The Company is to this day always in attendance on the reigning monarch while in residence at Holyrood

PRINCES STREET AND ELSEWHERE

28 *Princes Street from the West End, c.* 1903. St John's Episcopal Church is on the right, with the Scott Monument and the North British Hotel beyond. The vista is closed by the Calton Hill and its buildings

Writing for the first edition of his *Romantic Edinburgh,* published in 1900, John Geddie had this to say of Princes Street:

> 'Nor has Edinburgh, or its "New Town" much reason to complain if the impression of its beauty be drawn from the aspect and situation of the street which is at once its favourite promenade and the centre of its business life. "Her face is her fortune" someone had said of the Scottish capital; and if the High Street be the deep heart, Princes Street is the fair face of Edinburgh.'

The 'fair face' had lost its original and somewhat undistinguished symmetry of features by Victorian times, but nothing has been allowed to detract from the open aspect of the street despite a proposal to build at one time on its south, or garden, side. As in the case of the Royal Mile the photographs take a west to east sequence.

29 *(opposite)* *The Castle from the foot of Castle Street, c.* 1909

30 *St Cuthbert's Church* at the West End of Princes Street during the severe winter of 1888. This eighth-century religious site has had several churches on it, but only the spire of the building shown has any real antiquity. Former buildings succumbed to the ravages of the many sieges and defences of the Castle on its rock above, but the history of what has been called 'the oldest parish church in Scotland' is continuous to the present day

31 *The junction of Princes Street and Castle Street, c. 1910.* The 'area' shows how Princes Street, in common with adjacent streets, was originally constructed with cellars under the pavement

34 *(overleaf)* *Princes Street at the foot of the Mound, c. 1903.* The plans for the 'New Town' did not provide for the bridging of the marshy ground between it and the 'Old' and the Mound grew in the 1770s and 80s from the need of a convenient connection at this point. Much of the material came from foundation excavations in Princes Street and nearby. The four-in-hand 'brake' seen before the portico of the Royal Scottish Academy plied between the Waverley Market and the Forth Bridge

32 *A concert crowd in West Princes Street Gardens, c. 1907.* The buildings prominent on the skyline are the National Gallery, the Bank of Scotland and the Assembly Hall of the Church of Scotland

33 *East Princes Street Gardens and the Scott Monument, c. 1905.* From this point eastwards extended a complex of large stores and hotels; still there though now for the most part very much altered

35 *Princes Street at the foot of Hanover Street* as it was recorded in 1859 by G. W. Wilson, the Aberdeen photographer, on his first business visit to the capital. The rawness of the East Gardens which were then being laid out is clearly seen. George Meikle Kemp's monument to Sir Walter Scott did not long remain so open

36 *The East End from the Scott Monument* in 1880. The Calton Hill monuments on the skyline are the Observatory, the Dugald Stewart Monument, the National Monument, the Nelson Monument, in the shape of a telescope, the obelisk of the Martyr's Monument in the Old Calton burying ground and the turrets of the Gaol Governor's House

The National Monument was begun after the French wars as a memorial to the Scots soldiers who fell in the campaigns. It was intended to be a faithful reproduction of the Parthenon but funds ran out after the portion to be seen was completed. The foundation stone was laid during the period of George IV's visit to the city in 1822

37 *The East End and the buildings at the foot of the North Bridge, c.* 1872. The newly-completed Waverley Market with its rooftop garden is seen in front of the North Bridge buildings

38 *(opposite) The Waverley Bridge from East Princes Street Gardens, c.* 1870. Market Street runs along the front of the Cockburn Hotel and Cockburn Street winds upwards from the corner to connect with the High Street almost opposite the Tron Church, the steeple of which shows on the left

39 *Princes Street from the North British Hotel, c.* 1903. This view is in the opposite direction to No. 28. The Scott Monument is again prominent, but the spire at the far end of the vista belongs not to a Princes Street building but to St Mary's Episcopal Cathedral in Palmerston Place to which two other spires have now been added. The ladder method of boarding the 'Four-in-hand' coaches in the foreground must have been more than a little precarious for the ladies in the voluminous costumes of the day

40 *'The Iron Duke in Bronze by Steell'.* Wellington so approved of this statue by a native Edinburgh sculptor, Sir John Steell, that he had two copies made for erection elsewhere. At the unveiling in 1852 many veterans of the Peninsular and Napoleonoc Wars lined the steps of the Register House and more were present in the street to participate in scenes of great enthusiasm. There are many other monuments by Steell in Edinburgh, including the seated figure of Sir Walter in the base of the Scott Monument and the statue of Thomas Chalmers at the intersection of George Street and Castle Street

41 *An early photograph (c. 1854) of the East End* showing the Register House and Waterloo Place with a horse bus in the foreground

42 *The General Post Office, Waterloo Place and the Calton Hill, c.* 1902. The nearer horse tram in the foreground has sprung the points – a not unusual occurrence

43 *The 'Old' Theatre Royal, Shakespeare Square* taken in 1859 shortly before its demolition. This was the theatre against the raising of the walls of which George Whitefield had railed some 90 years before in terms of the ground and the building being 'appropriated to the service of Satan'

44 *The Register House from Waterloo Place, c.* 1905. The design of H.M. 'new' Register House is by Robert Adam and the foundation stone was laid in 1774. The records it contains include, in addition to the legal documents relating to land tenure, succession of heirs, etc., many important historical documents such as Scotland's copy of the Treaty of Union, the Act of Settlement of the Scottish crown upon the House of Stuart, the Declaration of Arbroath, 1320, and so on. It contains also the office of the Lord Lyon King-of-Arms

45 *Laying the Foundation Stone of the new North Bridge,* 25 May 1896. Twenty-three years earlier the original (1772) bridge had been widened by throwing out brackets to support the footways, so giving the maximum possible width to the roadway. But the continued heavy increase in traffic demanded still more drastic revision and widening at the expense of the remaining properties between this point and the High Street

46 *The Calton Hill, c.* 1905. The buildings are, left to right, the 'New' Observatory added to and enclosed by a wall ending in a memorial to his uncle Professor John Playfair, by the architect W. H. Playfair, who also designed the Greek style monument to the philosopher Dugald Stewart. To the right of the latter are the columns of the National Monument, referred to in No. 36, and the Nelson Monument. The ball on the top of the monument rises to the cross-shaft daily before one o'clock and falls again at exactly that hour, coinciding with the discharge of the One O'clock Gun from the Castle: except, that is, early in 1910 when it was held at the top by severe icing for six weeks. Below the Observatory and the Dugald Stewart Monument can be seen the studio and house of Alex. A. Inglis, photographer. This photographer's studio is one of the most famous in the world, having been occupied by D. O. Hill and Robert Adamson when they undertook their wonderful series of portraits of Church dignitaries and distinguished men which were to serve Hill as records for his painting of the 'Disruption of the Church of Scotland in 1843. It is only comparatively recently that Rock House, as the building was known, ceased to be a photographic studio

47   *Princes Street and the Old Town from the Calton Hill,* c. 1899. The building in the foreground is the Gaol or Bridewell on the site now occupied by St Andrew's House, the Scottish government offices

48   *A Circus Procession on the North Bridge,* 1901. The North British Station Hotel, under construction at the time (background), was completed and opened towards the end of 1902

49 *(overleaf)*   *The Waterloo Place, Calton Hill complex,* 1903. The roofs of the Register House and the General Post Office show in the left and right foregrounds, while Leith Street curves downwards to skirt the hill's north-westerly slopes where the square-towered Greenside Church can be seen

50, 52 *Shop fronts of two famous Princes Street stores* displaying a style of window-dressing no longer popular. The Mackay and Chisholm property, shown about 1905, is now occupied by one of the national multiple stores, while Darling's, owned at one time by one of Edinburgh's most famous twentieth-century Lord Provosts, the businessman and author Sir Will Y. Darling, is currently under redevelopment and will not be recognisable as the friendly shop which put out its welcome to King Edward in 1903

51 *George IVth Bridge and Bristo Street, c.* 1908. The New North Free Church established after the Disruption and opened in 1846 is now the non-denominational University Chaplaincy Centre. It has frontages to both Bristo Street and Forrest Road, just out of sight on the right. Beyond the Chaplaincy Centre can be seen the dome of the University's McEwan Hall

53 *Greyfriars Bobby.* Just out of the previous picture on the right this tribute to a faithful little terrier stands at the junction of George IV Bridge and Candlemaker Row. Eleanor Atkinson has written a very popular novel around his life of devotion to his master even after his master had been laid to rest in nearby Greyfriars Churchyard; and the faithful little dog's story has also been made into a film that had great success at the box-office. Bobby lay on or by his master's grave almost continuously until he himself died some hundred years ago in 1872. The photograph, taken about 1905 by A. A. Inglis (mentioned in No. 46), is one of many fine records of Victorian and Edwardian Edinburgh for which his camera was responsible

54 *The Flodden Wall, c.* 1906. One of the most complete remnants of the town wall built after the tragic battle of Flodden Field

55 *(opposite)* *The Denyston Tomb in Greyfriars Churchyard,* about 1846. David Octavius Hill, who is referred to also in No. 46, after composing the picture himself stood in on the left. Greyfriars Bobby's master's grave is not far from this spot

56 *The Union Canal near Fountainbridge, c.* 1910. The canal, completed in 1822, was designed to make a waterway connection between Edinburgh and Glasgow by joining up with the Forth and Clyde Canal near Falkirk. It was used successfully for heavy goods, including the stone for the Scott Monument, until the faster railway link overtook its usefulness. The footbridge in the picture was hand-operated when barges needed to get in or out of Port Hopetoun, the Edinburgh terminus. The site of Port Hopetoun is now occupied by streets, shops and offices and a cinema

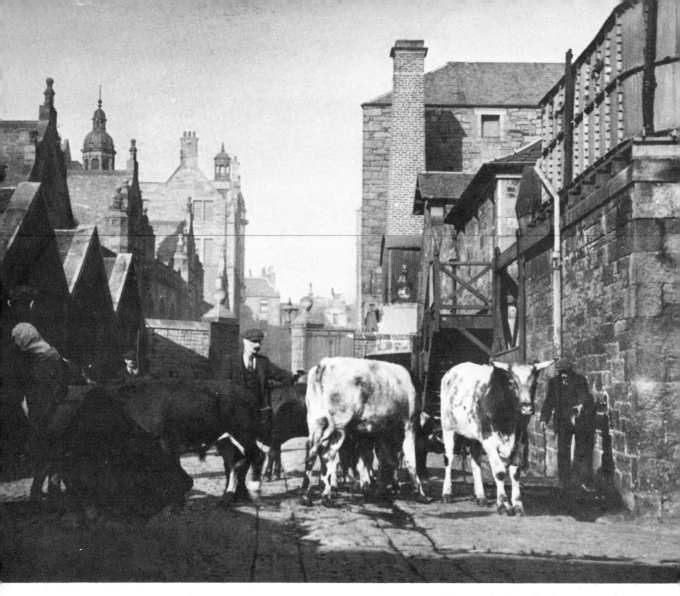

57 *The Slaughterhouse at Fountainbridge, c.* 1904. A meat market is still nearby, but its goods come from a newer abattoir in the suburbs

58, 60 *Schools Large and Small*. Two more contrasting and near-contemporary schools could hardly be found. The Wee School, Morningside is the Village School opened in 1823 and in use until 1895, while the High School in Regent Road, opened in 1829, served until moved to the suburbs in 1968. The High School became 'Royal' when King James VI conferred the title *Scholia Regia Edimburgensis* upon it near the end of the sixteenth century. During most of that century the school had been in borrowed premises the last of which was condemned in 1577 as 'nicht wattertycht, wyndtycht, nor lokfast'. As a result, the first purpose-built school was provided in 1578. The school in the picture is the third and was designed by Thomas Hamilton in the style and proportions of the Temple of Theseus at Athens. Other of Hamilton's works in his native city include the hall of the Royal College of Physicians in Queen Street, the Dean Orphan Hospital and the Burns Memorial near the School. Sir Walter Scott was a pupil from 1779 till 1783 or 1784 before going on to the University. Queen Victoria continued the royal connection with the school when she arranged for parts of the education of the Prince of Wales and the Duke of Edinburgh to be entrusted to the then Rector

59 *The corner of Leven Street and Tarvit Street, c.* 1903. A well-known shopping area for fruit, flowers and vegetables till cleared away to make room for the King's Theatre (opened 1906). Apples: 40 for 1/– !

61*(opposite)* *George Street at Hanover Street in 1867.* The statue is of George IV by Chantrey, the church is St Andrew's, erected in 1785. Here, in 1843, 470 members of General Assembly of the Church of Scotland being held within, walked out and proceeded to Tanfield Hall where the 'disruption' meeting referred to in No. 46 was held. The monument to Henry Dundas, first Viscount Melville, Lord Advocate in 1775 and holder of many offices under the Pitt administration is in St Andrew Square, the tall column having the proportions of Trajan's Column in Rome

60

62 *Victorian Ironwork Lamp and Drinking Well, Leith,* c. 1875. This fine specimen, which has now disappeared, was long an ornament to the foot of Leith Walk

63 *Foot of Leith Walk, 1898.* The lamp standard seen in the previous photograph is on the left, moved and somewhat modified, but it probably vanished in the general rebuilding of the Foot of the Walk that took place shortly after J. McKean took this photograph

64 *Great Junction Street, Leith, c.* 1906. The horse tram of No. 62 has been replaced by the Leith Tramway Company's new electric system introduced in 1905

65 *Bernard Street, Leith, c.* 1900. Less changed today than many Leith streets, it is still an important shipping office and banking centre, the Bank of Leith having been established here in 1806. During excavations in the street the course of a Roman roadway was uncovered

66 *Sheriff Brae, Leith, c.* 1907. Only the building on the left with the circular turret now remains

67 *The Shore, Leith,* in the 1860s. An early photograph showing the business of the Fish Market being carried on in the foreground

68 *The Inner Harbour and the Shore, Leith, c.* 1902. The old harbour Signal Tower is on the left

69 *The King's Landing, Shore, Leith, c.* 1905. Obscured by the ship lying alongside the Shore is the disembarking point where King George IV landed to begin his state visit to the capital in 1822

SOME 'CHARACTERS' AND FAMOUS SONS OF EDINBURGH

70 *Itinerant Match Seller,* whose principal 'pitches' were around the Lawn-market and Bank Street area

71 *'Bobbing Charlie'* snapped in Melbourne Place at the Midlothian County Buildings

72 *Match Seller* who stood at the Register House at the East End of Princes Street

73 *Sandy Malcolm,* the blind match, laces and pipe-top seller who used to sit at the Waverley Market railings on Waverley Bridge

74 *'Blind Kennedy'* with his dog Buller who led him to and from his station at the boundary wall of St Cuthbert's Churchyard, Lothian Road

76 *R. M. Ballantyne* (1825–94), author and amateur artist. Nephew of James Ballantyne, Sir Walter Scott's publisher, Ballantyne wrote some eighty tales for boys, including *The Coral Island,* and *The Young Fur Traders*

77 *Alexander Graham Bell* (1847–1922), inventor of the telephone. Bell removed with his father from Edinburgh to Canada in 1870 and became professor of Vocal Physiology at Boston University in 1872

78 *Henry Thomas Cockburn, Lord Cockburn* (1779–1854). Henry Cockburn wrote the invaluable *Memorials of His Time,* first published posthumously in 1856. There is no better guide to early Victorian society in Edinburgh

75 *(opposite)* 'Trawler Captain berthing his ship in Granton Harbour at the central pier. Taken after (immediately after) he had given a magnificent exhibition of seafaring language.' (Photographer's caption)

79 *Sir Arthur Conan Doyle* (1859–1930). The creator of Sherlock Holmes and Dr Watson, himself graduated in medicine at Edinburgh University before going into medical practice which he latterly forsook for authorship

80 *Kenneth Grahame* (1859–1932). In the 1890s Grahame wrote *The Golden Age* and *Dream Days,* studies of Victorian English country childhood, following them up in 1908 with the childrens' classic *The Wind in the Willows*

81 *Earl Haig of Bemersyde* (1861–1928). Field-Marshal Douglas Haig became Commander-in-Chief of the British forces in the First World War. Later he organised the British Legion and Poppy Day

82 *Sir Harry Lauder* (1870–1950). Scottish comedian and singer, wrote both words and music of many of his songs, including the ever popular 'Stop yer ticklin', Jock', and 'Roamin' in the Gloamin'

83 *William McGonagall* (1830?–1902), self-styled 'poet and tragedian', contributed much to the lighter side of Victorian social life in Dundee and Edinburgh with public and private recitals of his verses

84 *James Nasmyth* (1808–90), engineer, inventor of the steam hammer. Despite preoccupation with technical matters, Nasmyth found time for artistic activities including fanciful drawings which he humorously called 'shirtoons' as the proceeds were devoted to buying shirts

85 *R.L.S. Robert Lewis Balfour Stevenson* (1850–94), who himself adopted the 'Louis' spelling, was brought up to his father's profession of engineering. This having proved unsuitable for health reasons he turned to the law for a career, qualifying as an advocate in 1875. Before then, however, he had begun writing and in 1876 a series of brilliant essays contributed to the Cornhill Magazine won him high regard in literary circles. Books of travel and the adventure stories *Treasure Island, Catriona* and *Kidnapped* soon followed, and the great success of *The Strange case of Dr Jekyll and Mr Hyde* confirmed him in a career of authorship. Poor health eventually enforced exile from his beloved 'Hills of Home', the Pentlands, and after residences in the south of England and in France he settled in Samoa in 1889. The photograph is by his stepson and collaborator, Lloyd Osbourne

OCCASIONS

86 *The Edinburgh International Exhibition of Industry, Science and Art, 1886.* A feature of the Exhibition was the 'Old Edinburgh' section for which many features of the old town which had disappeared were reconstructed on the Exhibition site in the West Meadows. The photograph shows part of the 'Old Edinburgh' section on the opening day, with a reception committee lined up under a facsimile of the 'Blue Blanket', the banner of the Incorporation of Trades

87   *The Landing of the Czar Nicholas II and the Czarina at Leith, 22 September 1896 en route for Balmoral*

88, 92 *King George V and Queen Mary in Edinburgh, July 1911.* Their Majesties receiving a loyal address from the students of the University at the Students' Union. Processional Arch at the West End of Princes Street

89 and 90 *(overleaf)* *Visit of King Edward and Queen Alexandra to Edinburgh, 13 May 1903.* Princes Street decorated for the occasion and the Processional Arch at Minto Street

91 *Opening of the Imperial Dock, Leith, 8 November 1904*

GETTING ABOUT AND GOING PLACES

93 *Edinburgh's First Electric Tram*. Though the Leith system went straight from horse power to electric power about 1905, Edinburgh did not have its first electric vehicle until 1910 and that only operated between Ardmillan Terrace and Slateford. The trams had to be hauled to and from the depot by cable cars. The photograph was taken off-route in Princes Street in 1919 before even the overhead wires were in position

94 *Newington and Stockbridge Horse Bus.*
In the late 1850s, when this bus operated, it must have required some agility to ascend the vertical ladder to the back-to-back seating of the exposed top deck where the only safety feature consisted of a two- or three-inch high footrail. Three horses were needed to negotiate the steep gradients between Princes Street and Stockbridge

95 *Horse Bus,* c. 1896. Albert Street to Elm Row was one of the less hilly routes and required only two-horse traction

96 *The Last Horse Tram at Tollcross in 1907.* Horse trams, which began with a 'Tramways Act' in 1871 which authorised 'the laying of rails and the use of animal power only' were finally phased out when this tram made its last journey. The cabby, looking on, perhaps had mixed feelings as the 'mechanical monsters' of the cable car era were usurping much of his trade

97 *(overleaf)* *Cable Tram in Waterloo Place,* c. 1905. The cable system was noisy and breakdowns were not infrequent, but the leisurely 'jump on and jump off' possibilities were welcomed and made full use of by the more agile. The 'Four-in-Hand' out of town brakes in the distance had names such as 'May Queen', 'Rob Roy' and 'Queensferry Wanderer' instead of the more prosaic numbers of the car system

98 *Horse Trams*, 1905. Before the turn of the century rails were introduced on many routes to make the horses' task easier, especially in winter. Morningside and Portobello at that time represented the most southerly and easterly limits of the Edinburgh transport service

99 *Touting for Business outside a Railways Parcels Office, c.* 1860

100 *Early Motor Char-à-bancs, c. 1906.* The successor to the 'brakes' was the motor char-à-bancs (literally 'benched carriage'). There could have been little comfort on the 'benches' above those solid wheels!

101 *(opposite)* *Waverley Station, c. 1901.* The Down Main platform, cab rank and way out to the Waverley Bridge and Princes Street

102 *(overleaf)* *Commuters and Zoo visitors at Corstorphine Station, c. 1906.* This was the heyday of the suburban rail services

103 *Barnton Station, c.* 1909. The most westerly of the suburban stations, convenient for the players of the Royal Burgess Golfing Society and for excursions to Cramond and into the country by gig or on foot

104 *'Motorcade' for the Country, c.* 1902. Cars lined up for a run outside Craigcrook Castle near Blackhall, then in the possession of a well-known Edinburgh motor dealer and hirer

105 *Going Places?* Cabmen's Shelter, Balcarres Street, *c.* 1908, decorated for an occasion. The notice below the unflattering effigies of the happy couple reads: *In Morningside marriages are not rife; So Old Tam has ventured to take a wife; The honeymoon they say they mean; To spend it in Paris or Juniper Green.* The suburb of Juniper Green is some 680 miles the nearer!

106 *By Trap to Cramond Island, c.* 1895. The island is accessible to wheeled vehicles or on foot only for an hour or two on either side of low tide

WORK, LEISURE AND PLEASURE

107 *Fire Brigade at Exercise, c.* 1865. Testing a hydrant in George Street at the corner of St Andrew Square; Scott Monument in background

108 *Mussel Seller from Newhaven in Dundee Street*, near Lothian Road. The connoisseurs debate!

109 *Bellringer and Collecting Plate at Restalrig Church, c.* 1870

110 *Masons at Work at the Foundations of the Scott Monument in Princes Street, c.* 1843, one of several fine photographs of the subject by Hill and Adamson

111 *Masons at Work raising the height of the parapet of the Dean Bridge (c. 1910?). This action followed a number of suicides and was taken as a precaution by the authorities*

113 *(opposite)   The Lamplighter. A later 'leerie' than the one in R. L. Stevenson's poem. My tea is nearly ready and the sun has left the sky; It's time to take the window to see Leerie going by; For every night at teatime and before you take your seat, With lantern and with ladder he comes posting up the street. A Child's Garden of Verses, 1885*

112 *Parade of the Operative Bakers' Society of Scotland in the King's Park, c. 1910. 'The Staff of life' in many of its forms*

114 *(overleaf) Laying Granite Setts between Tramlines at the Foot of Leith Walk, c. 1905*

115 *Newhaven Fisher Boys.* A study, c. 1846, by Hill and Adamson (see No. 46)

116 *Feeding Time at Swanston, c.* 1900. Photograph by John Patrick

117–118 *Newhaven Fishwives at work and at leisure, c. 1906*

119 'The Trivial Round, the Common Task' on Cramond Island in the 'nineties

120 Wash Day at Balerno, c. 1900   121 (opposite) Farm Cottage Kitchen, Cramond Island, 1895

122   *A Town Gossip in the Canongate, c. 1907*

123   *Street Ventriloquist in the Grassmarket, c. 1908*

125 *Italian Organ Grinder and his monkey in Belgrave Crescent, c. 1910*

126 *A Day at the Seaside, Portobello Sands, c. 1909*

127 *Gymnastic Club*, 1891. The group includes three amateur boxing champions of Scotland – lightweight, middle-weight and heavyweight

128 *The Heart of Midlothian Football Club*. The team of 1875–76 in the original 'Hearts' strip

130 *Professional Golfers on Leith Links,* 1867. Tom Morris, first winner of the British Open Championship, is playing the shot. His son, 'Young Tom', who won the 'Open' three times in succession 1868, '69 and '70 to win the original trophy outright, is in the centre wearing light trousers. Willie Park, in light suit, another 'Open' winner, looks on at the left

131 *Town Get-Together in a West End bar, c.* 1910

132 *Country House Party at Broomfield, near Davidson's Mains, c.* 1894. Sir John Murray, of the 'Challenger' oceano-graphic expedition, the centenary of which was celebrated in 1972, is the gentleman with the child on his shoulders. The photographer was Professor George Chrystal, author of a famous textbook on algebra

133 *Swing Park in the East Meadows, 1908*   **134** *(opposite)*   *Pleasure Sailing from Leith, c. 1910*

135 *A Day at the Zoo;* feeding the bears, *c.* 1909

136 and 137 *(opposite)* *Portobello Pier and Donkeys on the Sands, c.* 1906

138 and **140** *(overleaf)   Temporary Pleasures at the 1908 Scottish National Exhibition in Saughton Park.* The 'Moulin Rouge' Helter Skelter and the Conference and Concert Hall

139 *(opposite)   Pleasure Interrupted:* a booking for stealing 'tumchies' (turnips), *c.* 1911

140

OPEN SPACES

141   *Duddingston Loch, c.* 1908: feeding the Swans

142 *Camera Club Outing to Blackford Glen* between the Blackford and Braid Hills, *c.* 1870

143 *Braidburn Valley, c. 1907; bringing in the hay*

144 *Haymaking at Swanston, c. 1902*   145 *(overleaf)* *Boating at Portobello, c. 1910*

146 *The River Almond at Cramond, c.* 1900. Edinburgh's western boundary is formed by the river for some miles upstream

147 *Swanston, 1900;* R. L. S.'s 'Hills of Home'. The scree-faced hill on the right is Caerketton which lies above Swanston Cottage, the Stevenson home. *Be it granted to me to behold you again in dying, Hills of home! and to hear again the call; Hear about the graves of the martyrs the peewees crying, And hear no more at all.* R. L. Stevenson, 'To S. R. Crockett'

OLD VILLAGES, SUBURBS AND SURROUNDINGS

148 *Causewayside and the Grange Toll, c.* 1854. The Toll House is by the white houses on the left. The open gutters were a feature of the streets of the period

149 *Echo Bank, c.* 1860. The hamlet of Echo Bank was in part demolished in 1886 to make way for the row of villas fronting Newington Cemetery on the Dalkeith Road

150 *High Street, Portobello, c.* 1905. Portobello, largely a development of the late eighteenth and early nineteenth centuries, was notable principally during Victorian and Edwardian times as a bathing resort, first of the well-to-do and later popular with all levels of society. Later still the sands were perhaps at their busiest in summer during the annual Glasgow Fair holidays. The origin of the rather curious name is attributed to a Scottish sailor who had served with Admiral Vernon at the siege of Puerto Bello, Panama, in 1739. His 'Portobello Hut' was built on the Figgate Muir in 1742

151 *The Village of Blackhall, c.* 1865. No more than a hamlet on the way between Edinburgh and the Queen's Ferry at the time this photograph was taken, only rudimentary traces now remain in the modern suburb

152 *St John's Road, Corstorphine, c.* 1905. Corstorphine (the derivation of the name is obscure) was already more than a village when brought into the city by the provisions of the 'Boundaries Extension and Tramways Act' of 1920 and has now extended far beyond the limits of the photograph

153 *The Tram Route from Portobello to Levenhall at Levenhall, c.* 1904

154 *Forth Bridge mania invades the photographer's studio.* Enthusiasm for the bridge in the 'nineties was tremendous and this was one expression of its popular appeal